# Hawai'i's Road to Statehood

**CORNERSTONES OF FREEDOM**

SECOND SERIES

Deborah Kent

**Children's Press®**
A Division of Scholastic Inc.
New York • Toronto • London • Auckland • Sydney
Mexico City • New Delhi • Hong Kong
Danbury, Connecticut

Photographs © 2004: AP/Wide World Photos: cover top, 40; Bishop
Museum Archives: 31; Bridgeman Art Library International Ltd.,
London/New York/The Stapleton Collection: 14; Brown Brothers: 17;
Corbis Images: 4, 8, 29, 35, 44 top, 45 top left (Bettmann), 41 (Royalty-
Free), 12, 15, 28, 39, 45 bottom; Culver Pictures: 3 (E.M. Newman),
cover bottom, 13, 21, 23, 24, 26, 44 bottom left; Hawaii State Archives:
5 bottom, 16; ImageState/Richard Pharaoh: 6, 45 top right; Library of
Congress: 37; Mary Evans Picture Library: 10; Naval Historical Center,
Washington, DC: 30; North Wind Picture Archives: 5 top, 7, 9, 11, 18, 19,
20, 22, 25, 27, 44 right, 44 bottom center; PictureHistory.com: 36; Stock
Montage, Inc.: 32, 33; Time Life Pictures/Getty Images/Myron Davis: 34.

Library of Congress Cataloging-in-Publication Data
Kent, Deborah.
  Hawaii's road to statehood / Deborah Kent.
      p. cm. — (Cornerstones of freedom. Second series)
  Includes bibliographical references and index.
    ISBN 0-516-24241-5
    1. Hawaii—Juvenile literature. [1. Hawaii—History.]
I. Title. II. Series.
  DU623.25.K46 2004
  996.9—dc22

                                             2003023890

CHILDREN'S PRESS, and CORNERSTONES OF FREEDOM™, and
associated logos are trademarks and or registered trademarks of
Scholastic Library Publishing. SCHOLASTIC and associated logos
are trademarks and or registered trademarks of Scholastic Inc.

1 2 3 4 5 6 7 8 9 10 R 13 12 11 10 09 08 07 06 05 04

O N A BALMY JANUARY DAY in 1893, Queen Lili'uokalani of Hawai'i hosted a reception at her royal palace. She had invited all of Hawai'i's legislators, or lawmakers, to attend. About half of the legislators were native Hawaiians, people of Polynesian ancestry. The rest were haole, white-skinned people of European or American descent. As the legislators looked on, a band of native Hawaiians streamed through the palace gates. Their leader carried a new constitution, or set of governing laws. The queen intended to put the new constitution into effect right away.

## THE LAST QUEEN OF HAWAI'I

Lydia Kamaka'eha was crowned Queen Lili'uokalani of Hawai'i in 1891. Her movement to restore the power of the monarchy took the motto "Stand Firm." She was overthrown in 1893 and held prisoner in her home for the next five years. A haunting song written by Lili'uokalani, "Aloha 'Oe," is one of the best-loved songs in Hawai'i today.

This portrait of Queen Lili'uokalani was taken in 1887.

This new constitution would overturn the Constitution of 1887, which had been forced on the **monarchy** by wealthy haole. The 1887 constitution had strengthened the hold of the haole over the Hawaiian Islands. The queen hoped that the new constitution would restore the monarchy to its former power.

Despite the queen's careful planning, however, two of her trusted Cabinet members refused to sign the new constitution. Outraged, the queen announced that the grand signing ceremony would be delayed. Her supporters threatened to riot.

* * * *

Meanwhile, haole leaders gathered to take action. They decided that the time had come to overthrow the monarchy and put Hawai'i directly into the hands of the United States. To support this plan, 162 fully armed sailors and marines came ashore from a U.S. warship anchored near Honolulu, Hawai'i's capital. The ship's cannons loomed, ready to open fire on the city. The queen and her supporters saw that resistance would lead to disastrous bloodshed.

On the afternoon of January 17, 1893, haole leaders declared that the Kingdom of Hawai'i was no more. They announced the creation of a provisional, or temporary, government. It would be headed by an American named Sanford Dole. The haole hoped and believed that the United States would **annex** Hawai'i as soon as the news reached Washington, D.C. This meant that Hawai'i would no longer be an independent nation. It would be a territory of the United States.

Sanford Dole was the first president of the Republic of Hawai'i.

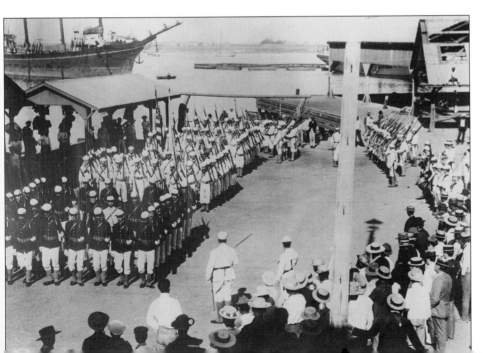

In 1893, United States Marines arrived in Hawai'i to force the surrender of the Hawaiian kingdom to the United States.

5

The islands of Hawai'i have beautiful beaches and lush tropical landscapes.

# THE LOVELIEST FLEET OF ISLANDS

Hawai'i has long captivated visitors with its coral reefs, sandy beaches, and rugged volcanic mountains. Writer Mark Twain described Hawai'i as "the loveliest fleet of islands that lies anchored in any ocean." Another American writer, Joaquin Miller, declared, "I tell you, the man who has not seen the [Hawaiian] Islands, in this one great ocean's warm heart, has not seen the world." Novelist Jack London stated simply, "Hawai'i is a song."

Hawai'i is a chain of 132 islands splashed across the North Pacific about 2,390 miles (3,846 kilometers) southwest of California. Most of the islands are uninhabited **atolls**, or rings of coral surrounding saltwater lakes called

* * * *

lagoons. The eight major islands are Ni'ihau, Kaua'i, O'ahu, Moloka'i, Lana'i, Mau'i, Kaho'olawe, and Hawai'i. The island of Hawai'i is sometimes called the Big Island because it is the largest in area. Honolulu, the capital and largest city, is on the island of O'ahu. O'ahu has been the most densely populated island in the Hawaiian chain since 1900.

Human beings first settled Hawai'i around A.D. 300. These first settlers came from the Marquesas Islands in Polynesia, an area in the South Pacific. Another group from the Polynesian island of Tahiti arrived about five hundred years later. These two groups of Polynesian peoples mingled to form the tall, broad-shouldered native Hawaiian race. The Hawaiians were a gracious, friendly

**Hawaiians dance for an audience.**

people who enjoyed singing, dancing, surfing, and other physical activities. Each island was ruled by one or more chiefs, or *ali'i nui*.

The first European to write a detailed description of Hawai'i was the British captain James Cook. Captain Cook landed on Kaua'i in January 1778. He named the islands

Explorer James Cook and his crew were the first Europeans to visit Hawai'i. He was welcomed with gifts and ceremony.

After a time, the actions of Cook and his crew angered Hawaiians. A fight eventually broke out between the two groups. Cook was killed in 1779.

the Sandwich Islands in honor of the Earl of Sandwich, who helped pay for his voyage. Cook and his crew arrived during a festival for Lono, the Hawaiian god of the harvest. At first, some of the Hawaiians thought that the white-skinned strangers might be gods and that their leader was Lono himself. They treated Cook and his crew to two weeks of feasting, dancing, and song.

Cook set sail again, but returned to Hawai'i a year later. By now the Hawaiians suspected that the visitors were human beings after all. Tensions began to mount. The strangers ate up the Hawaiians' reserves of food and had no respect for their ancient religious customs. Violence flared when Cook kidnapped the ali'i nui of the island of Hawai'i. In the fight that followed, Captain Cook was killed.

**Ships sailing the Pacific found that Hawai'i was a good place to stop for supplies.**

# A COLLISION OF CULTURES

As the years passed, ships from Europe and the United States often anchored at the Hawaiian Islands. Whalers and merchant ships stopped to take on water and other provisions. Soon Hawai'i played an active role in the world of trade. The Hawaiians sold **sandalwood** from island forests in exchange for rum, guns, and other goods.

These newcomers brought more than trade goods to Hawai'i. They also carried a host of infectious diseases that the Hawaiians had never encountered before. The Hawaiians had no natural resistance to protect them from measles, smallpox, tuberculosis, and other illnesses that were widespread in Europe and North America. The ships also brought diseases from Asia, including bubonic plague and **leprosy** (known today as Hansen's disease). One epidemic after another swept through the islands. Historians estimate Hawai'i's population at more than five hundred thousand when Captain Cook arrived. A century later the native Hawaiian population was down to only sixty thousand.

In 1810, King Kamehameha I united the eight major islands and founded the Kingdom of Hawai'i. Kamehameha was an intelligent and determined chief. He ruled for nine years, struggling to retain native values and traditions despite the growing influence of foreigners. He also adopted some foreign ways that he hoped would make the kingdom stronger.

King Kamehameha I united the people of Hawai'i. He was known as a wise ruler during his reign from 1810 to 1819.

### THE FAIRY-TALE KING

The story of Kamehameha I's childhood is surrounded by legends. In 1758, a dazzling comet appeared in the skies over Hawai'i. Prophets claimed that the comet foretold the birth of a new chief who would defeat every rival. When a son was born to a Hawaiian chief, the chief's enemies ordered the baby killed. According to legend, the baby was rescued and raised in secret. Historians find no truth in these stories. Yet the tales show that the Hawaiian people held Kamehameha in very high regard. He is often called Kamehameha the Great.

**A missionary preaches in the shade of kukui trees.**

In addition to guns and rum, newcomers from the United States brought Christianity to the Hawaiian Islands. The first Christian **missionaries** arrived from New England in 1820. With tireless energy, they worked to convert the Hawaiians to their strict Protestant faith. The missionaries built churches and opened schools. They developed a writing system for the Hawaiian language and translated the Bible and other religious materials. They also concerned themselves with Hawaiian clothing, or lack of clothing. In the hot, humid climate of the islands, Hawaiian women traditionally went topless. Men wore only a cloth around their hips. The missionaries encouraged the Hawaiians to cover their bodies in American-style dress.

The missionaries also influenced Hawai'i's royal family to practice a more **democratic** form of government. In 1840, Hawai'i created its first constitution. It was modeled after the Constitution of the United States, and it set up a government with a supreme court and a two-house legislature. The United States recognized Hawai'i as an independent nation in 1842.

### THE HAWAIIAN ALPHABET

Until the coming of the missionaries, the Hawaiian language had no written form. The missionaries developed a Hawaiian writing system using twelve English letters. Hawaiian uses the five English vowels and seven consonants: *H, K, L, M, N, P,* and *W.*

This photograph shows the first mission building in Honolulu, around 1870.

## A LAND OF RICH DIVERSITY

During the nineteenth century, Americans and other foreigners began to buy large areas of land in the islands. The **descendants** of New England missionaries became wealthy landowners. Some of these landholding families experimented with cattle ranching. Cowboys from Mexico came to Hawai'i to brand calves and herd steers.

In the 1850s and 1860s, haole landowners established sugarcane plantations. California was an eager market for sugar from Hawai'i. Many hands are needed to plant, tend,

**This photograph shows a boat filled with cattle on its way to Hawai'i in the 1890s.**

and harvest sugarcane. Many more must take it to the mills
and turn the raw sugar into a product that could be sold. At
first, the planters relied on the labor of the native Hawaiians. They soon faced a problem, however. Haole plantation
owners argued that there simply were not enough Hawaiians
to do all the necessary work.

A new law, passed in 1850, opened the way for a differ-
ent kind of workforce to enter Hawai'i. The Act for the
Governance of Masters and Servants allowed landowners
to bring in **indentured** laborers from other countries.
Under the indenture system, the employer paid a worker's
ship passage and other traveling expenses. The worker
was then bound to the master for at least three years in

15

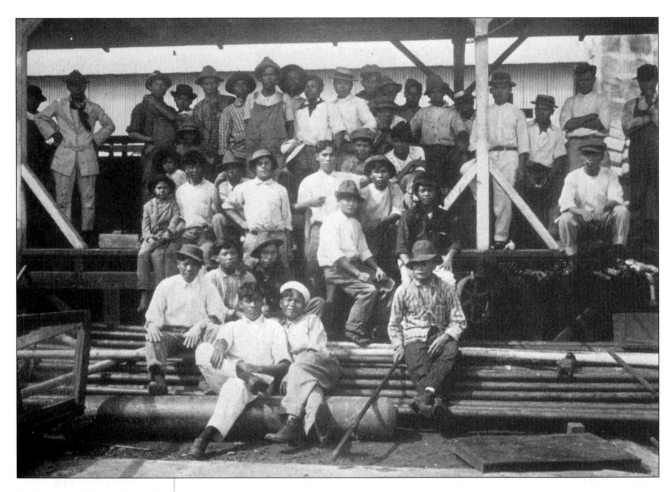

**By the early 1900s, Hawai'i's labor force was made up of people from a wide variety of ethnic backgrounds, including Japanese, Spanish, Portuguese, and Filipinos.**

order to pay back this debt. If a worker left the plantation before his indenture was complete, the police hunted him down and put him into prison. Critics argued that the indenture system was a form of slavery. The sugar planters ignored these objections, despite the fact that their parents and grandparents had worked so hard to bring democracy to Hawai'i many years before.

At first, nearly all the laborers who came to Hawai'i under the indenture system were men from China. Later, workers from Japan, Puerto Rico, Polynesia, and the Philippines signed indenture contracts to work in Hawai'i's sugarcane fields.

As contracts expired and workers gained their freedom, they left the plantations to enter a wide variety of careers and professions. Hawai'i became a nation of rich diversity. One American journalist visiting the islands in 1873 described a village school: "On the benches sit, and in the classrooms recite, Hawaiian, Chinese, Portuguese, half white and half Chinese children; and the little pig-tailed [Chinese] reads out of his primer as well as any."

In 1874, Hawai'i's King Kalakaua visited Washington, D.C. He was the first reigning

## HAWAI'I'S SOCIAL SCALE

Hawai'i had a rigid social system, with one group above another like rungs on a ladder. The haole were at the top. They controlled most of the land and money. Below them ranked the native Hawaiians. Still lower on the scale came the Chinese. The Japanese were ranked at the very bottom of the social order.

Hawaiian schools included children of many backgrounds, among them native Hawaiian and Japanese, shown here.

monarch of a foreign nation ever to visit the United States. The king spoke to both houses of Congress and met with President Ulysses S. Grant. Because of the king's visit, the United States and Hawai'i signed an important treaty the following year. The U.S. removed a **tariff**, or import tax, on Hawaiian sugar. This meant that Americans could buy sugar from Hawai'i more cheaply, ensuring plantation owners a steady market. In return, Hawai'i promised to buy certain goods only from U.S. merchants. In 1887, the rights of the United States were strengthened even more. A new treaty allowed the U.S. to dock naval vessels at Pearl Harbor in Honolulu.

**King Kalakaua traveled to Washington, D.C. in 1874. He was the first ruling king to visit the White House.**

**This crowning ceremony for King Kalakaua and Queen Kapi'olani was held at 'Iolani Palace in 1883.**

King Kalakaua believed that the monarchy needed to gain the respect of foreigners by having Hawaiian symbols of dignity and strength. In 1881, he ordered the construction of 'Iolani Palace, a splendid mansion for the royal family. The costs of the palace and a fabulous ceremony to crown the king and queen caused the country to go into debt.

Haole businessmen decided that the king was unfit to rule. In an armed rebellion they forced him to sign a new constitution in 1887. Because this document was forced

President Grover Cleveland believed that the overthrow of the Hawaiian monarchy was "an act of war." He later said that the only honorable course of action would be to restore power to the native Hawaiians.

upon the king and his people, it is sometimes called the **Bayonet** Constitution. The Constitution of 1887 stripped the king of most of his power. It was a step in the haole master plan to make Hawai'i part of the United States. It was this constitution that Queen Lili'uokalani had hoped to undo at her reception in 1893. Her plan did not succeed, and the Kingdom of Hawai'i came to an end.

## THE CHANGING OF THE FLAGS

When the haole abolished the kingdom in 1893, they hoped that the United States would annex the islands. To their dismay, U.S. president Grover Cleveland disapproved of the events that had taken place in Honolulu. He described their action against the queen as "an act of war against a

* * * *

friendly nation." Cleveland refused to annex Hawai'i to the United States. He also urged that the queen be restored to her throne.

The haole paid no attention to the president's advice. Instead, they set aside the provisional government and drew up a new constitution. The former kingdom became the Republic of Hawai'i. Hoping to win the acceptance of the native Hawaiians, the Republic of Hawai'i continued to fly the eight-striped flag that had been the symbol of the Hawaiian kingdom.

The United States went to war with Spain in 1898. During the Spanish-American War, the U.S. government felt a growing need to establish a naval base in the Pacific Ocean. American ships had used Hawai'i's Pearl Harbor for decades. Now the navy wanted to make the harbor into a fueling station for ships in the Pacific Fleet.

## MAKING AMENDS

In 1993, the U.S. Congress passed Public Law 103-150, known as the Apology Bill. The bill is an apology by the U.S. government for the overthrow of the Kingdom of Hawai'i in 1893. Some Hawaiians regard the Apology Bill as a step toward Hawaiian independence. They believe that Hawai'i should become a sovereign nation once again.

This photograph shows a view of Honolulu Harbor around 1870.

A new president, William McKinley, did not share Cleveland's doubts about annexing Hawai'i. Hawai'i's president, Sanford Dole, invited Congress to annex the young republic. The response was enthusiastic. Five years after the fall of the monarchy, Congress voted to make Hawai'i a U.S. territory. Former president Cleveland wrote sadly,

> *Hawai'i is ours. As I look back upon the first steps in this miserable business and as I contemplate the means used to complete the outrage, I am ashamed of the whole affair.*

Wealthy members of the haole community in Hawai'i were overjoyed when they learned of Congress's decision. Territorial status was a step toward statehood. Native Hawaiians, on the other hand, were upset by the idea of annexation. The haole were already trying to stamp out

**This photograph shows the last Cabinet meeting of the Republic of Hawai'i before annexation by the United States in 1898. Sanford B. Dole is seated in center.**

Hawaiian natives feared that their traditions would soon be lost as a result of annexation.

their customs and language. At school, children were beaten if they spoke Hawaiian instead of English. The Hawaiians feared that gaining statehood would make matters even worse. Some 37,000 Hawaiian women and men signed a **petition** addressed to the U.S. Congress. The petition read in part:

> *We particularly resent the presumption of being transferred to the United States like a flock of sheep, or bartered like a horde of savages, . . . and we cannot believe our friends of the great and just American nation could tolerate annexation by force against the wishes of the majority of the population.*

**This photograph shows American troops near Pearl Harbor in 1894.**

In truth, however, the native Hawaiians were a minority in their own country. They were far outnumbered by people who had come to Hawai'i from distant lands such as China, Japan, the Philippines, Portugal, Great Britain, and the United States. Overwhelmed by these groups, the voices of the native Hawaiians were barely heard.

On August 12, 1898, a joyful haole crowd filled the grounds of 'Iolani Palace, now known as the Executive Building. A band played the Hawaiian national anthem, and warships in the harbor sounded a twenty-one-gun salute. Slowly the Hawaiian flag was lowered on its staff. As the yards of fabric sank to the ground, piercing wails tore the air. The palace was filled with the soulful cries of hundreds of Hawaiian women who had gathered in a nearby church. The wails of mourning formed a grim background as the official ceremony proceeded. The band broke into the

A crowd of haole celebrate the news of annexation.

★  ★  ★  ★

This drawing by J. Steeple
Davis shows the American
flag being raised for the
first time over the
Executive Building.

national anthem of the United States, "The Star-Spangled Banner," and the Stars and Stripes rose above the palace.

The Hawaiians grieved for the end of their monarchy and the loss of their independence. As time passed, however, Hawaiians reluctantly accepted that the islands were bound to the United States. Some began to see statehood as their hope for the future.

## ROADBLOCKS

By an act of Congress, in 1900, Hawai'i's status as a U.S. territory became official. Hawaiians were now U.S. citizens. The U.S. president appointed Sanford Dole as Hawai'i's first territorial governor.

### TERRITORIAL STATUS

When Hawai'i became a U.S. territory, its people became American citizens. They did not have the full rights of U.S. citizenship, however. They could not vote in presidential elections. And although they could elect a representative to Congress, he or she was not allowed to vote on bills (proposed new laws) or other issues. Hawaiians could also vote for their own legislators, but the president of the United States appointed the governor of the territory.

With great ceremony, Sanford B. Dole was inaugurated as the governor of Hawai'i on June 14, 1900.

Many Chinese people in Honolulu settled in part of the city that became known as Chinatown, pictured here in 1908.

Most citizens of the territory, especially the haole, assumed that Hawai'i would soon join the United States as a state. Territorial status had long been a step on the road to statehood. A territory need only reach a population of 60,000 citizens, write a constitution, and apply to Congress for admission as a state. Hawai'i had a population of about 150,000 and was growing steadily year by year.

The makeup of Hawai'i's population, however, troubled the members of Congress and the American people. More than half of all the people in Hawai'i were Asians of Chinese or Japanese origin. About one quarter were either native (Polynesian) Hawaiians or part Hawaiian. There were few haole in Hawai'i, even though they controlled most of the wealth. They accounted for only 17 percent of the territory's population.

In the early 1900s, much of Hawai'i's land was used to harvest the territory's top two sources of revenue—pineapples and sugar.

Fear and mistrust of Asians ran strong in the United States. China and Japan were not Christian nations. Asians did not have white skin or European facial features. In addition, they were often willing to work for low wages. People in the United States were afraid that Asian immigrants would take jobs away from American workers. Congress was unwilling to admit Hawai'i to the Union because of its large Asian population.

Though the United States refused to admit Hawai'i as a state, it had no doubts about opening military bases on the islands. In 1908, the U.S. navy dredged, or deepened, the entrance to Pearl Harbor and set up an important base of operations there. The first naval vessel to

### HAWAI'I AND THE PINEAPPLE

In 1899, a pioneering businessman named Jim Dole introduced a new crop to Hawai'i—the pineapple. Pineapples quickly became a major **export**, second only to sugar. Jim Dole was the brother of territorial president Sanford Dole.

enter the new harbor was the USS *California*. To mark the occasion, the *California* carried two honored guests, Sanford Dole and former queen Lili'uokalani.

The loyalty of Asian residents was a concern to many Americans. In times of war would Chinese Americans and Japanese Americans stand by their new country? American citizens of every ethnic background proved their loyalty in 1917, when the United States entered World War I. Thousands of young men from Hawai'i rushed to enlist in the American armed forces. On the home front, territorial citizens sold war bonds to support the United States and its allies.

**The USS *California* is escorted into Pearl Harbor on December 18, 1911.**

A clipper "flying boat" flies over O'ahu in 1935.

In 1918, when the war was over, the people of Hawai'i thought they had earned statehood at last. Prince Jonah Kuhio, Hawai'i's nonvoting representative in the U.S. Congress, introduced a bill calling for Hawaiian statehood. Kuhio's bill was sent to committee for study. It received little attention and finally died.

Improvements in transportation brought Hawai'i closer to the United States. Air travel between Honolulu and Los Angeles became a reality in 1935. Instead of a five-day journey by ocean liner, passengers could now reach Hawai'i on a sixteen-hour flight. The ties between Hawai'i and the United States seemed closer than ever before.

★ ★ ★ ★

Arriving by airplane, a group of U.S. congressmen visited Hawai'i for twelve days. The citizens of Hawai'i welcomed the senators and representatives. They greeted them with **leis**, performed traditional dances in their honor, and took them on a tour of the islands. The congressmen concluded that Hawai'i met all of the requirements for statehood. However, they went on to recommend "further study."

The story was the same two years later, when a second group of congressmen visited the islands. By then, Japan was building up its military strength and had launched an invasion of China. The world was on the brink of another war. The U.S. was more cautious than ever about admitting a new state with a large Japanese population to the Union.

## GO FOR BROKE!

By 1941, about two-thirds of the U.S. Pacific Fleet was docked at Pearl Harbor. Some people worried that Pearl Harbor might be a target for a Japanese attack. The navy prepared for war. When bombers swooped over Pearl Harbor on the morning of December 7, most people in the territory thought that the

This photograph captures the scene at Pearl Harbor just moments after the attack.

navy was staging a practice drill. Honolulu families hurried toward Pearl Harbor to watch the excitement. But the bombers were not American planes. On their wings they bore the Rising Sun, the **emblem** of Japan.

## IMPRISONED WITHOUT TRIAL

At the start of World War II, the U.S. government had no evidence that Japanese Americans were disloyal. Yet the government suspected that they might be spies. In 1942, President Roosevelt ordered that all Japanese Americans on the West Coast of the United States be moved to detention camps. Some 112,000 people of Japanese ancestry were forced to leave their homes and live in camps surrounded by barbed wire and guarded by armed soldiers. About 1,400 Japanese Americans from Hawai'i were sent to detention camps, where they remained until the end of the war.

Personal belongings are sorted at Heart Mountain, a detention camp in Wyoming for Japanese Americans. From 1942 to 1945, about 14,000 Japanese Americans passed through Heart Mountain.

The two-hour attack caused terrible destruction. More than 2,400 people died. Eighteen naval vessels and 188 planes were destroyed. Most of the dead were U.S. servicemen, but sixty-eight **civilians** also lost their lives. Hawai'i's governor, Joseph Poindexter, put the territory under martial law. This meant that the military had complete authority over territorial citizens. The military imposed martial law in an effort to protect the territory from further enemy attack and to prevent any anti-American activity from occurring on the islands.

* * * *

The following day, U.S. president Franklin D. Roosevelt declared war on Japan. Germany's Adolf Hitler declared war on the United States three days later. For the next three and a half years the United States was embroiled in World War II, which lasted until 1945. Throughout the war years Hawai'i served as the main base of operations for U.S. forces in the Pacific. The population of Hawai'i nearly doubled from the number of incoming servicemen and supporting personnel.

At the beginning of the war, about 40 percent of all people in Hawai'i were of Japanese heritage. Many Japanese families had lived there for generations. Second-generation Japanese in the islands were known as Nisei. Most Nisei thought of themselves as Americans and citizens of the United States.

Eager to prove their loyalty, about 2,800 Japanese Americans from Hawai'i enlisted in the U.S. army after the Pearl Harbor attack. They formed the 442nd Regimental Combat Team, which eventually joined the 100th Infantry Battalion.

A group of Japanese Americans in Hawai'i anxiously await their turn to sign up for service in the American armed forces during World War II.

A company officer of the 442nd Regimental Combat Team teaches new recruits how to salute.

## FROM DICE TO THE BATTLEFIELD

The motto "Go for Broke" came from a dice game popular in Hawai'i. When a player bet all his winnings on a single throw of the dice, he announced, "I'll go for broke!"

The 100th/442nd fought bravely in Italy and other parts of Europe. So many men in the 100th/442nd were wounded in battle that it was nicknamed the "Purple Heart Battalion." The soldiers of the 100th/442nd fought with everything they had. Their motto was "Go for Broke!"

## STATEHOOD AT LAST

After World War II, the people of Hawai'i were more determined than ever to join the Union. In 1950, voters expressed

* * * *

their overwhelming support for a new state constitution. Yet again Hawai'i's efforts to become a state were blocked.

This time the roadblock was a surging fear of communism that swept the United States in the early 1950s. In Hawai'i, seven people who were accused of being communists were charged with trying to overthrow the U.S. government. They were arrested in 1951. Most of the "Hawai'i Seven" were labor organizers or journalists. They had fought for improved working conditions for plantation workers and the longshoremen who loaded ships on Hawai'i's docks. Though they posed no real threat to the U.S. government, all of the Hawai'i Seven were found guilty. The long and public trial of the Hawai'i Seven again fueled doubts that citizens of Hawai'i deserved to be full citizens of the United States.

At Hawai'i's Constitutional Convention in 1950, delegates gathered to write a constitution for Hawai'i. They hoped that statehood would be approved.

* * * *

For many territorial citizens the prospect of statehood gleamed with promise. They imagined that statehood would bring an end to the inequalities and injustices of life in the islands. A professor at the University of Hawai'i wrote,

> *Hawai'i's admission to the Union as the forty-ninth or fiftieth state will be the symbol that Hawai'i's social structure has attained the characteristics of American society. It will [foreshadow] the disappearance of minorities, Oriental, Hawaiian, and Haole.*

Hawai'i's bid for statehood was finally linked to that of another U.S. territory, Alaska. John A. Burns, Hawai'i's delegate to Congress, reached an agreement with the Alaskan delegate. Both territories petitioned for statehood at the same time. Burns believed it would be hard for Congress to reject them both or to admit one without accepting the other.

Burns's strategy proved to be successful. In 1958, Congress approved a bill to make Alaska the forty-ninth state in the Union. Hawai'i's bill was passed by the Senate on March 11, 1959, and by the House of Representatives on March 12. President Dwight D. Eisenhower signed Hawai'i's statehood bill on August 21, 1959. Hawai'i became the fiftieth state to join the Union.

All over Hawai'i people poured into the streets. Bells rang, sirens blared, and bands played "The Star-Spangled Banner."

President Dwight D. Eisenhower (center) declares Alaska's statehood on January 3, 1959. Hawai'i would soon follow.

The Stars and Stripes flew from balconies and rooftops. Hawai'i's long journey to statehood was finally at an end.

Statehood did not, of course, turn Hawai'i into an earthly paradise. Inequalities persisted, as they do nearly everywhere. A boom in tourism from the mainland brought jobs

★ ★ ★ ★

**Young people in Honolulu celebrate the news of statehood in March 1959.**

and money to the islands, but it also caused new problems. High-rise hotels and condominiums sprouted along once-pristine beaches. Forests were felled to make room for highways and shopping malls. Dozens of species of native Hawaiian birds and plants disappeared forever. Sometimes clouds of smog darkened the skies over Honolulu.

On March 13, 1959, the day after Congress approved Hawai'i's statehood, a crowd gathered in Honolulu's Kawaiaha'o Church. Reverend Abraham Akaka, a native Hawaiian, said,

✳   ✳   ✳   ✳

*There are some of us to whom statehood brings great hopes, and there are some to whom statehood brings silent fears. One might say that the hopes and fears of Hawai'i are met in statehood today. There are fears that statehood will motivate economic greed toward Hawai'i, that it will turn Hawai'i into a great big spiritual junkyard filled with smashed dreams—that it will make us lonely, confused, insecure, empty, anxious, restless, disillusioned—a wistful people.*

Then he reminded his listeners of an ancient Hawaiian chant. He repeated its words in English, assuring the crowd that Hawai'i's spirit would live on: "There is salvation for the people, for now the land is being lit by a great flame."

**Honolulu is now a big, bustling city with tall buildings and highways.**

# Glossary

**annex**—to attach a region to another state or nation

**atoll**—ring-shaped coral island surrounding a lagoon

**bayonet**—a knife that can be attached to the end of a rifle and used as a weapon

**civilians**—nonmilitary citizens

**democratic**—relating to government by the people or by elected representatives

**descendants**—people who are related to those who came before them

**emblem**—official symbol

**export**—goods sold to a foreign country

**indentured**—bound by contract

**leis**—flower necklaces traditionally offered to visitors in Hawai'i

**leprosy**—disease that leads to deformities of the face and limbs; also known as Hansen's disease

**missionaries**—people sent to another place to spread their religion

**monarchy**—government headed by a king or queen

**petition**—document signed by many concerned citizens, pleading for a cause or making a public statement

**sandalwood**—fragrant wood native to Hawai'i

**tariff**—tax on goods brought in from another country

# Timeline: Hawai'i's Road

| 300–500 | 800–1000 | 1778 | 1810 | 1840 | 1842 | 1887 |
|---|---|---|---|---|---|---|

The first human settlers reach Hawai'i from the Marquesas Islands in Polynesia.

Hawai'i is settled by another group of Polynesians from Tahiti.

British captain James Cook lands at Kaua'i and names the islands after the Earl of Sandwich.

Kamehameha I unites the eight major islands and founds the Kingdom of Hawai'i.

The Kingdom of Hawai'i adopts its first constitution.

The United States recognizes Hawai'i as an independent nation.

In an armed uprising, King Kalakaua is forced to sign a new constitution that weakens the monarchy.

# to Statehood

Queen Lili'uokalani is overthrown by the haole; the Republic of Hawai'i is established.

The United States annexes Hawai'i.

Hawai'i becomes a U.S. territory.

Prince Jonah Kuhio introduces a bill for Hawaiian statehood to the U.S. Congress.

Territorial citizens approve a new constitution to be submitted to the U.S. Congress.

**MARCH 12** Congress approves a bill to grant Hawai'i statehood.

**AUGUST 21** President Dwight D. Eisenhower signs the bill, making Hawai'i the fiftieth state in the United States.

The U.S. Congress passes the Apology Bill, in which the federal government apologizes for the overthrow of the Kingdom of Hawai'i in 1893.

# To Find Out More

## BOOKS

Dowswell, Paul. *Pearl Harbor: December 7, 1941*. New York: Raintree/Steck-Vaughn, 2004.

Johnston, Joyce. *Hawaii*. Minneapolis, MN: Lerner Publications, 2001.

Morrison, Susan K. *Kamehameha: The Warrior King of Hawai'i*. Honolulu: University of Hawaii Press, 2003.

Sherman, Josepha. *Queen Lydia Lili'uokalani, Last Ruler of Hawai'i*. Carolrhoda Books, 2004.

## ONLINE SITES

The Hawaiian Historical Society
*www.hawaiianhistory.org*

Ehawaiigov
*www.hawaii.gov*

Aloha—Hawai'i.com
*www.aloha-hawaii.com*

# Index

**Bold** numbers indicate illustrations.

# About the Author

**Deborah Kent** grew up in Little Falls, New Jersey, and received a bachelor's degree in English from Oberlin College. She earned a master's degree from Smith College School for Social Work and worked for four years at the University Settlement House in New York City. She wrote her first young-adult novel, *Belonging*, while living in the town of San Miguel de Allende in Mexico.

Kent is the author of more than a dozen novels and numerous nonfiction titles for young readers. She lives in Chicago with her husband, children's author R. Conrad Stein, and their daughter, Janna.